L2

THE
COUNTRYSIDE
REMEMBERED

THE COUNTRYSIDE REMEMBERED

SADIE WARD

FOREWORD BY
GORDON BENINGFIELD

CENTURY

London Sydney Auckland Johannesburg

Picture research, editing and design
by Jill Hollis and Ian Cameron

Produced by Cameron Books,
PO Box 1, Moffat, Dumfriesshire DG10 9SU

First published in 1991 by Century,
an imprint of Random Century Group Limited,
Random Century House,
20 Vauxhall Bridge Road, London SW1V 2SA

Random Century Australia Pty Ltd,
20 Alfred Street, Milsons Point,
Sydney 2061, Australia

Random Century (NZ) Ltd,
18 Poland Road, Glenfield,
Auckland 10, New Zealand

Random Century South Africa Pty Ltd,
PO Box 337, Bergvlei, 2012 South Africa

A catalogue record for this book is available
from the British Library

ISBN 0 7126 5053 9

Filmset by Cameron Books, Moffat
Printed in The Netherlands by Royal Smeets
Offset, Weert

Cameron Books is grateful to the Institute of
Agricultural History at the University of
Reading for permission to reproduce the
photographs in this book which are taken
from its extensive photographic holdings,
with the exception of the pictures on the
following pages: 53 (top) Mary Evans; 56 (top),
66, 67, 88-89, 90 (top and bottom), 91 (top)
Popperfoto; 56 (bottom), 57, 58, 59 (bottom),
62, 69 (bottom) Hulton-Deutsch Collection.

The author wishes to acknowledge the help
and advice of Bill Petch.

Illustration: a scene on an angora rabbit farm
near Littleton-on-Severn, Gloucestershire, in
1935. The farmer tended the rabbits while his
mother spun their wool.

FOREWORD

The pictures in this book call up powerful memories for me. As a boy, in the 1940s and 1950s, I spent a great deal of my free time working on farms near St Albans in Hertfordshire. Luckily, the village school I went to had a very understanding headmaster, and when the two weeks we were allowed off to help in the fields at harvest time stretched a bit, he mainly let me get away with it. If I hadn't become an artist, I would certainly have worked on the land, though I probably wouldn't have lasted long because I wouldn't have been able to tolerate the way things were changing.

What I remember was a mixture of sheer hard work and treats. On a winter's day, picking frozen mangelwurzels out of the ground could be so painful that it made you cry with the cold, but at other times, like harvest time or hay-making, there were pay-offs. The farm hands we worked with wouldn't tolerate slacking or messing about. The day's work had to be done. Of course, some farmers were not as good to work for as others, but on a reasonable farm there was a lot of camaraderie when you weren't working.

People relied a lot on what was available at certain times of year. You looked forward, say, to new potatoes, apples, collecting rosehips from the hedgerows for rosehip syrup and blackberries for blackberry and apple pie. I still remember the real excitement that went with getting an unplucked cockerel straight from the farm for a special occasion like Christmas. My grandmother used to pluck and dress it. Now you can get pretty much anything all the year round and it doesn't seem special any more.

There is now a totally different attitude to work on the land. We have destroyed the love of the countryside among those who work in it. What farmworker sitting inside the cab of a noisy machine going up and down over enormous areas of prairified fields can hear the first cuckoo of the year or take the time to notice that the bluebells have suddenly carpeted a wood nearby? You have only to look at the faces of farmworkers today and you can tell there is no appreciation of their surroundings and little satisfaction in what they do. Their lives are sheer drudgery. In the old days, skill and craftsmanship were everywhere, whether in the expertise of the wheelwright or in the ability of the labourer to turn his hand to thatching a rick. It is easy to see why people often had such a pride in their work. They were also resourceful. If they needed a bit of timber for, say, fencing, they wouldn't go off to the local timber yard or DIY store, but would use what they could find, like the spare branches left over after laying a hedge.

But now specialisation means that there is little variety in the everyday tasks on a farm, and many people may find themselves with jobs that are as monotonous as a shift on a production line. In the old days, farms were a hive of activity and gangs of mates kept each other company while working. That kind of companionship is just not there any more. There may be only two workers on a farm and, in any case, the noise of heavy machinery precludes contact.

Wages were low, but there were compensations. Lots of cheap milk, free logs, lots of things you could pick up, such as rabbits – most farmers were only too pleased to have a few taken off their land. Nowadays, many farmworkers wouldn't know the difference between a blackberry and a rosehip – their contact with the countryside and the seasons has been almost completely broken. That sort of knowledge is now pretty much irrelevant.

The involvement of country dwellers in the cycle of the seasons and the traditional farming year was so strong that memories of it are still very close to the surface. It provided a kind of rhythm and source of satisfaction that is just not to be had now. If you are very lucky, you can find traces of this lifestyle, still surviving, in the south west of England. But it has mainly gone for ever. How sad that so many people now yearn for something that we have got rid of as recently as the last forty years.

So much that is in this book was still really familiar to me in the 1950s, and I was not living in some remote backwater but in the Hertfordshire countryside only thirty miles from London. Although many of the images recall the sheer hard work of it all, perhaps this book will be a reminder of how much the countryside can offer if it is treated with respect.

Gordon Beningfield

Water End
Hertfordshire
June 1991

INTRODUCTION

Over the years since the start of the Second World War, the landscape of Britain has changed almost beyond recognition. The countryside as we see it now reflects the transformation that has taken place in almost every aspect of farming.

The great appeal of traditional mixed farming lies in the natural balance and harmony of the whole system. Arable land produced not just food crops but also fodder for the stock, whether cattle, sheep or pigs. The animals were run on grassland or 'folded' on arable fields between the main crops, producing dung which sustained the fertility of the soil. The crops were grown in rotation to preserve the viability of the land. All this made for a landscape of great variety – a patchwork quilt of different textures and hues expressing the ever-changing pattern of the farming year.

Before the war, though, agriculture was in a state of depression at the end of a slow decline that stretched back to the late 19th century, and farmers were finding it difficult to make a living. But in wartime, necessity dictated that Britain should become as nearly sufficient in food as was possible through the mobilisation of every resource. A vast acreage of pasture land was ploughed up in the campaign to feed the nation, and food production has continued to rise ever since, way past the early expectations of either farmers or governments.

The old system of husbandry which had been developed over the centuries relied on a combination of horse and hand power for most farm work. After the Second World War the move towards mechanical power accelerated, but for a while it was quite common for both tractors and horses to be seen working together in the same field. The younger men took to the tractor enthusiastically. It allowed them to work sitting down, it was quicker and it was 'modern' – there were newly acquired skills to show off. Some older men took a more nostalgic view: they had enjoyed the company of their horses and had taken a pride in their ploughing.

By the 1960s, the farm seemed a much lonelier pace. A key reason for mechanisation was that while machines were expensive to buy and maintain they slashed labour costs, which meant that there were many fewer people on the land. Because the machinery is at its most efficient on large, uninterrupted areas, the hedges, trees and ditches that once separated small fields have been removed – in some parts of the country a single field may be as large as a whole farm was a hundred years ago. And the fields have been made smoother since the combines and other machines do not work well on land that lies in the ridges and wide open furrows created by the usual type of horse-drawn plough.

In the interests of profit, modern farming favours specialisation in either crop or livestock production, particularly in lowland regions. Great expanses of southern and eastern England have been turned over to almost continuous crops of wheat and barley, the latter mainly for malting and as a concentrated food for intensive beef production. Yields have been increased by heavy applications of chemical fertilisers and by chemical sprays to control weeds and insect pests. Advances in plant breeding have provided farmers with improved and more resistant varieties. The heavier, healthier and more uniform crops that result give the landscape a well-manicured appearance, and many of the downlands of southern England have become a great sheet of corn with scarcely a weed to be seen. But it was these very weeds that gave the fields much of their colour – spraying has almost done away with the poppies, cornflowers and corn cockles and even with the farmer's bane, charlock, the bright yellow flowers of which are now hardly to be seen among the green corn. The hedgerow flowers have disappeared along with the hedgerows themselves; the crops now go right to the edges of the fields and the gateways are kept clear of the daisy-like mayweed which sixty years ago contributed to an impression of pleasing unkemptness. Now the main splash of colour in the spring countryside comes from the garishness of the rape fields with their shattering yellow flowers – rape is grown for its seeds which are crushed and included in animal feeds.

Haymaking has become much less common. Grass, now grown with high doses of nitrogen (which gives it a distinctive dark green colour) is cut in May or June for silage. But the nitrates which are applied to the soil in such quantities are easily leached out by rain and may end up polluting rivers; other chemicals such as phosphates, which are relatively immobile in the soil, may build up to a level that affects plant species that once coexisted with agriculture. Certainly the herb-rich meadows so beloved of those who treasure the wealth of Britain's wild flora have all but vanished.

Gone, too, are many of the familiar sights. Perhaps the most romantic in retrospect were those associated with the corn harvest, which few people under thirty will have seen: the fields dotted with orderly rows of stooks, the sheer numbers of hands needed to bring in the harvest, the beautifully thatched corn ricks in the corner of the field or in the stack yard awaiting the attentions of the threshing gang. The actual threshing, to separate the grain from the straw, was usually done in the winter months, often in the pre-war days by hired steam contractors who brought with them what by today's standards was a huge range of equipment: a threshing machine, a steam engine to drive it and a water tank to feed that, an elevator to help in building the straw into a stack after threshing, a source of power for the elevator and, last but not least, teams of horses and wagons to take away the sacks of corn. Today the people, horses and equipment involved in the hugely labour-intensive tasks of harvesting and threshing have been replaced by the combine harvester with its single driver which cuts, threshes and cleans the grain in one operation. Then mechnical balers gather the staw into the bales of square, rectangular or round section and increasingly large size that now dominate the landscape of late summer.

Free-range livestock was still a common sight on farms throughout the 1950s. However, the switch to intensive animal production had started as long ago as the 1920s and 1930s, when the first specialist poultry farmers began to use battery farming techniques and a few entrepreneurs invested in so-called Pig Palaces. Modern equivalents of these are now the rule, and even sheep may be kept indoors over the winter months to keep them in good condition so that they can lamb safely. Grazing cattle are less often seen nowadays in lowland arable districts – they are spending more of their increasingly short lives indoors and in yards. Many of the new livestock houses were built with distinctive tower silos for storing feed, but as the cost of these carbuncles has risen, there has been a trend towards storing silage in equally unattractive stacks covered with black plastic and old tyres. Meanwhile the older farm buildings have fallen into decay and been demolished or turned into workshops or smart residences, often for newcomers to the countryside, many of them commuters or weekend visitors. Instead of the old cowsheds, barns and granaries built in such traditional materials as cob and thatch, brick or stone, there are standardised structures of concrete and steel, almost always more efficient but often eyesores that at best can be camouflaged with a screen of greenery.

It is easy to romanticise the era when so much was done using time-honoured techniques. But much farmwork was backbreaking and very hard, with long hours in the summer and having to be out in wet or freezing conditions in the winter. Even working in traditional farm buildings such as cow byres or stables might be far from pleasant. as they would have been unheated and have had little natural light. For all his toil, the farmworker had little financial reward, being then, as now, at the bottom of the national pay ladder, and the few perks he did enjoy, such as a probably very primitive farm cottage, were small compensation.

Certainly it is neither desirable nor possible to turn the clock back to the era of unmodernised farming. Yet there was much to be valued in the old system of mixed husbandry with its inherent sustainability. Although it was suitable only for some areas of the country and did require purchased inputs such as seeds and chemicals, its strength lay in the perfect integration between the various operations on the mixed farm, an integration that extended beyond the farm to the local rural economy that revolved around it.

Ironically, farming is once again facing depression; the developments of the past fifty or sixty years have also left it with a problem of overproduction – Britain now produces three times as much wheat and twice as much milk as it did in 1939. There is concern about both the surpluses and the environmental damage that can be attributed to intensive farming. One way forward that has been suggested is through financial inducements to farmers to work in a more environmentally sensitive way, for example by reducing the quantity of chemicals they use and generally farming in a less costly way to produce a lower output of food – this is called extensification. Perhaps some of the older methods of farming depicted in this book will have a new validity and can be reinterpreted for the future. The day of the horse and hard manual labour has gone, but the lesson of sustainability may be as essential for the next century as it has been in the past.

The Countryside Remembered does not set out to provide any sort of comprehensive historical account of life in the British countryside. Rather, it presents a collection of images chosen to evoke the rich and varied texture of rural life as it had long existed in Britain and which survived to well within living memory – although some of the photographs in this book date from the 1930s, the majority are from the 1940s and 1950s, with even a few from the early 1960s.

Horse power

Horses and men labouring together on the land – a sight that now seems as primitive as it is romantic, but which could still be seen as recently as the early 1960s. These three photographs were taken during the second half of the 1950s.

The ploughman's job was a highly skilled one. In the photograph below, the perfect rhythm of the team of horses – Darky, Toby and Nobby – has been caught as they 'dance' on the headland, turning for the next run down a field near Gravesend in Kent. The reversible plough, used here, turned the soil one way on the outward trip and the other way on the return trip, producing a more even surface than the open furrows associated with ordinary ploughing. This was better for the modern implements that would be used later in the year: binders, for example, would not break so readily on level land. And it was also safer for the sheep which might later graze on this kind of field; on open furrowed land, they could easily trip, roll over on their backs and be unable to get up again.

A windswept plough-team in Dumbartonshire. It is difficult to see whether a single or double-furrow plough is being used. For medium and light soils, a double-furrow plough, although requiring more skill and strength, was the more efficient, but stiff land often needed single furrow treatment.

North Country farmers preferred 'drilling on ridges' while their counterparts in the south tended to drill (put in the seed) on the flat. Here, on Corporation Meadows near Berwick-on-Tweed, some beautifully drawn ridges are being rowed up with a ridging plough, ready for drilling with swede. Elsewhere in the field, there might well be a team of women spreading artificial fertiliser by hand before the seed is put in.

A well-deserved midday break for a winter plough team is being taken in the photograph below. Typically, the horses would have been taken out at about seven in the morning, worked until around nine and then given a short break but no feed. Work would have continued without another pause until noon, when both ploughman and horses would stop for an hour's rest and something to eat. They would then be ready for the afternoon stint. By four-thirty, or sometimes earlier, if the light was going, they would be back in the stable. The horses' nosebags, usually made of cocoa matting and manilla hemp, probably contain oats and chaff, and the ploughman is almost certainly eating bread and cheese. His puttees, probably old kit from the Great War, make it likely that this photograph was taken in the early 'thirties.

Between the First and Second World Wars, agricultural horses were still the main source of power on the farm; many farmers considered them to be more economical than a tractor for a variety of farmwork as well as for general carting and haulage. The extra power of the tractor was useful for really heavy jobs, such as ploughing, drilling and cutting corn, although horses were still better for lighter work where a great deal of stopping and starting was involved (as in loading corn sheaves into

wagons before the advent of the combine harvester).

    During the depression years, a great deal of arable land reverted to pasture and this, plus the trend to mechanisation, reduced the need for agricultural horses. Even so, there were still 650,000 of them in harness at the outbreak of World War II. Often horses and tractors were used complementarily, a horse-drawn harrow following a tractor drill, for example. This may well have been the case where this photograph was taken, near Chelsham in Surrey, where a zig-zag harrow is being run over the ground to cover the seed after barley has been drilled – light horses for a light job.

Muck-spreading on a cold winter morning in Kent, January 1952. Next the ploughman will have the hard task of ploughing in both dung and an unsold crop of rotting cauliflowers. It was not until 1939 that artificial fertilisers were used in any quantity. Until then, farm manure was supplemented by horse dung brought back from the towns, but supplies dwindled as motorised transport took over from horse power.

Looking after working horses is a specialised task. On an estate or large farm, the head horseman or carter might have several assistants, right down to a young ploughboy, who would not yet have had a team of his own. The carter's authority was absolute, and he ranked high in the farm workforce. On a small farm, one of the general labourers might have had to manage the horses as well as doing his normal job. This became more common in the 1930s as farmers looked for ways of reducing their wage bills. Opposite: plough teams returning from work at Preston Hill in Wiltshire in the 1930s, led by the head horseman, whose day is far from over. The horses must still be taken out of harness, groomed, fed and watered. On the left, the horse drinking is in trace harness, which probably means that he was harnessed to another horse for work, and his companion is in cart harness for shaft work.

Steam-powered engines were the embodiment of the Industrial Revolution on the land. Although their heyday was past, they lingered on between the wars, chiefly for threshing and barn work, but still sometimes for cultivation, where their enormous power could be put to tackling tasks impossible for horses or the available tractors. They could, for example, be put to ploughing up particularly heavy clay soils, and in a dry summer a steam engine could come into its own breaking up land which had been put down to grass for a few years. But steam power was expensive and much of the work was done by contractors travelling with

their machinery from farm to farm within a locality. In 1918, some 600 steam ploughing sets were in use, but by 1938 this had declined to 125.

Shown below is a traction engine driving a chaff cutter, which is chaffing hay (cutting it into small fragments) to feed to pedigree store cattle on a group of estate farms near Tring in Hertfordshire in 1928.

Opposite is a steam cultivator at work on a farm near Pulborough in Sussex in 1934. The 16-ton ploughing engine is one of a pair, positioned on either side of the field, and the cultivator is hauled across the field between the two by means of a steel

cable running from a winding drum under the boiler on each machine. The engines move forward along the headland as the work proceeds.

On the right is an early internal combustion-engined 1917 International Harvester Titan – one of the most popular of the American tractors imported during the Great War – which ran on paraffin. It is drawing a Wilder Pitch Pole to aerate the soil. The great advantage of this piece of equipment, with its different sets of tines for arable and pasture land, was that it was self-cleaning: as one set of tines became clogged, a pull on the tripcord would bring another into play, while the first was cleaned by the movement of the equipment. Like many such museum pieces, the tractor was brought out of retirement in the Second World War; it was acquired in 1944 for £25 to help with another wartime plough-up campaign.

Winter feeding

Traditionally, beef cattle were expected to grow and gain weight cheaply on grass from early spring to autumn, and then were fed rations of one sort or another in winter. But winter feed was often not particularly nutritious and many animals tended to lose weight, so were not ready for slaughter until they were at least two-and-a-half years old.

From the 1880s, attempts were made to produce feed suitable for sustaining and even fattening beef cattle over the winter months.

But since the last war, the quest for ever more efficient methods of turning cattle into meat has led to increased feeding of stock on grain-based concentrates to produce so-called barley beef – animals that spend much of their short lives in purpose-built housings and yards in a system which in its most extreme form is (somewhat euphemistically) called 'zero-grazing'.

In the 1920s and 1930s the extra nutrients needed by overwintering cattle would have come from dry stuff (such as hay) and sliced or pulped roots, together with concentrated feeds such as grain and oilcake, but as farmers became less able to afford the careful hoeing and weeding needed to cultivate root crops, they began to depend more on silage made from grass, clover or lucerne.

The cattle in two of these pictures are spending their winter days outside, and feeding them is hard, cold work. On the left, hay is being provided for a herd of Red Polls at Little Compton in Oxfordshire, while the Shorthorns in the snowy landscape are being given some kind of succulent feed – possibly kale, cabbage or other green fodder. They would probably have been brought back to the farmyard at night to conserve energy and produce dung which could be mixed with straw to supply manure for the farm.

Even in the days of traditional farming, cattle could spend monotonous winters almost entirely in unlit buildings – as on this modest holding photographed in 1961 near Okehampton in Devon. By the early spring, when they are turned out to grass, the Devon calves will have spent months in almost complete darkness, without any mucking out, on a diet of milk supplemented by hay and concentrates.

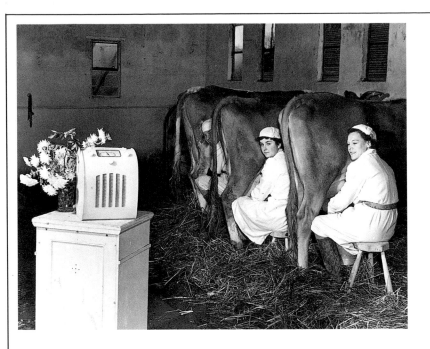

Milking

This idyllic scene, with its rickety footbridge and untrimmed river banks so close into the village, is at Longparish in Hampshire in the 1950s. It was a common sight in the era of mixed farming, when many small farmers kept a few dairy cows. Now the herds are larger and fewer but, at least in Britain, dairy cattle are still put out to graze on grass in the summer and brought in for milking two or three times a day.

Before the war, it was common to keep cows in cowsheds over the winter months, and to milk them more or less traditionally. But now almost all farmers have gone over to the system of loose housing or yarding in which the cows can feed themselves from a stack of silage, the dung can be removed by machine and the cows are mechanically milked in a milking parlour.

The milkmaids were photographed in 1951, when farmers still did not have to guarantee that their milk reached a specific standard in order to sell it. But the Milk Marketing Board (set up in 1933) ran incentive schemes to encourage higher quality production and more attention to cleanliness, offering a bonus to farmers who would guarantee the quality of their milk, and granting them a license to produce graded milk which meant that they could charge higher prices. These milkmaids, with their impressively clean uniforms, have been taught not to put their heads against the cows' sides, to avoid dust falling into the milk.

Once collected from the farms, milk that was destined to supply relatively far-flung destinations was transported by rail – here the milk churns are being despatched from Aysgarth station in North Yorkshire to London. Around the time that this photograph was taken in 1929, London received about 100 million gallons of milk a year by railway. The train here is probably a passenger train with a few separate milk vans. Milk specials generally left late in the evening or at night and arrived in time for the next day's first delivery of milk.

Pigs

All of these photographs were taken in the 1950s, when many general farmers still fitted inexpensive open-air pig-keeping in with other activities on the farm. On the whole, sows were tethered on arable land or grassland or put in runs with their litters, for fear that they would harm piglets that were not their own. Every few days, they would be moved with their portable shelters to clean ground. Sometimes a herd was allowed to forage more widely, which helped to reduce feed costs. Below is a winter field being cleaned up in short order (note the movable shelters in the background) and opposite, a boy, no doubt earning some pocket money, watches over a number of Saddleback sows and their litters as they graze a harvested field for fallen ears of corn – one of a number of tasks that even the under tens in a farmer's family were expected to help with. The Middle White sow lying so contentedly in the sun in the farmyard, with her typically dished, upturned face, earned a caption in 1956 that to modern ears has a poignant sound: 'On a farmyard – anywhere'.

Poultry

Many small farmers continued to keep a few hens for the table well into the 1960s, and their wives regarded the 'egg money' – from selling eggs at market – as a useful supplement to their house-keeping. Where they were kept in any quantity on mixed farms, poultry were typically treated as part of the general cropping programme, being moved periodically to clean

land, together with their cheap, portable housing, having grazed and manured the preceding section. Although semi-intensive and intensive methods of production (first introduced in the 1930s) were well-established by the 1950s, many farmers still kept birds in relatively free-range conditions. The Aylesbury ducks, photographed as they emerge from foraging in sodden grass and mud beneath blackcurrant bushes, are seven-week-old table birds on a poultry farm at Speldhurst in Kent in 1955, and the turkeys are a small flock from a total of 160,000 turkeys bred for the Christmas table near Chesham in Buckinghamshire in 1959.

Field work

Although by the early 20th century the usual method of sowing seed was to drill it by machine, broadcasting by hand was still used on small farms, especially where the ground was hilly or awkwardly shaped, or to undersow a crop or thicken it after normal drilling. The seed would be held in a sack or seedlip – a woven or covered basket – or in a container made of thin wooden boards or galvanised iron. Here a particularly long bout of severe weather in 1947 had held back ploughing and sowing, and the ground was still too water-logged for mechanical drilling. Considerable skill and natural rhythm were required: if the hand and foot on the same side were not thrown together, the ground would not be evenly covered. Ideally, steps should be short, the cast frequent and the pace steady, so that it could be sustained throughout the day's work.

Above is one of the endless back-breaking tasks that were involved in raising field crops of vegetables, in this case, Brussels sprouts, near Pershore in Worcestershire in 1956. The seed, which was put in with a hand-pushed drill, has come up thickly, and each plant must be pulled individually and loaded into boxes. The same women might well then transfer to work on a tractor-drawn transplanter, which set the young plants back into the ground at intervals.

To modern eyes, the enormous scale of tasks tackled by hand and the sheer numbers of people involved in just one stage of cultivation – here planting seed potatoes – are impressive. Usually the potatoes would be dropped into the furrows, but in this case extra care has to be taken because the tubers have sprouted. The seed has to be covered quickly, so that it cannot be damaged overnight by late frosts. The horses, drawing a ridging plough, have been trained to walk on the ridges rather than in the newly planted furrows. Left: a typical planting gang – made up of local women and their children on a farm near Aberuthven in Perthshire – put in early potatoes in April to be ready for lifting by late July. By the time this picture was taken, in 1951, children under thirteen should not, strictly speaking, have been employed, but many often 'helped' for pocket money.

Right: a huddle of workers dropping in Red King potatoes, which, unlike the 'earlies', were not lifted until they ripened in September, unless market conditions were favourable. Lifted when their skins had set, they were stored in clamps for sale later. Below, a pre-war planting scene, showing the encroachment of suburbia on the market-garden areas that surrounded the great conurbations. These women would have been paid about four shillings a day.

By the 1950s, mechanisation was being introduced into fieldwork, but a large number of
labour-intensive tasks still remained. Village
women were taken on for a variety of seasonal
farm tasks such as planting, singling and hoeing as well as hand-picking various crops. Here
beet is being singled near Blewbury in Berkshire. Women were generally reckoned to be
superior to men wherever nimble fingers or
meticulous work were required. Male farm
workers and the women usually worked in
separate groups; the foreman was unlikely to
approve of the distractions from hard labour
offered by mixed teams. Reliable gangs were
hard to come by and farmers tended to get
together and agree on a fixed rate per day so
that there was little temptation for gangs to
break up and seek work elsewhere. These labourers would have worked between 8.30 a.m.
and 4.30 p.m. for about sixteen shillings a day.

By 1958, when these thistle dodgers were photographed in Sussex, most growing corn was sprayed with liquid weed killer, but here a traditional method of lifting thistles with an ancient tool called a spud is in progress. An old East Sussex doggerel ran: Spud them in May/They are up next day./Spud them in June/They come again soon./Spud them in July/When they will soon die.

Below, a fill-in job on a West Riding farm in May 1945 after the spring work was over and before haymaking: stones are being collected to save the mower in a field of meadow grass.

One of the jobs at which women were said to be much quicker and more proficient than men – pea-picking, here in the fields at Sandy, Bedfordshire, in July 1939. At this time 70,000 acres in Britain were devoted to peas to be 'picked green', and all the work was done by hand. Harvesters have now been developed which run over the standing crop and remove the peas in a single operation.

Market peas were cleared at one picking by gangs, who often had to be imported from neighbouring towns because of the number of labourers required, especially on large farms in the Eastern Counties. The farmers provided transport and the pickers were paid on a piece-work basis.

Opposite: the local women from North Fleet in Kent have turned out to gather in a war-time spring onion crop. As they are wearing

wellingtons, they are probably experienced field workers – the boots could be obtained only with a permit from an employer, a restriction which led Land Girls to complain bitterly about the difficulty of getting adequate footwear for fieldwork. Children under school age had to spend long days in the fields with their mothers if there was no neighbour or relative to look after them.

The harvesting of onions and root crops such as potatoes and carrots has now been entirely mechanised. But despite the best endeavours of plant breeders and agricultural engineers, some species simply do not lend

themselves to mechanical harvesting: crops such as runner beans have to be picked frequently if yield and quality are to be kept up; others – like strawberries – would run too great a risk of damage. Most of the brassicas – cabbage, cauliflower, broccoli – are still hand-harvested, although there is now a system for harvesting Brussels sprouts semi-automatically. Opposite, on a farm near Plympton, South Devon, in 1937, a record harvest of Savoy cabbage is being despatched daily in pot hampers to London and other city markets. The hemp bags were probably for Brussels sprouts and the standing sacks contain potatoes.

This photograph, taken in the 1930s near Harpenden in Hertfordshire, shows watercress beds being cleared of weeds in preparation for the summer crop. Watercress can be grown successfully only on suitable sites and these are not easily found. The most extensive areas have always been in chalk and limestone districts, usually in valleys where natural springs supply clear, uncontaminated water. Many watercress beds fell into disuse after 1945 because they were uneconomic; in the 1970s and 1980s there was a revival, but now for the limited, though high-value market in hotels and supermarket chains. The harvesting of watercress is now completely mechanised.

The lupins in this 1930s photograph are being grown as cut flowers near Chichester in Sussex. Until relatively recently the selection of flowers was mainly limited to what was available in season from the local market garden or nursery. Nowadays, a large proportion of the cut flowers available in British shops is imported, principally from Holland, and huge advances in horticultural technology have enabled previously seasonal blooms to appear all the year round.

Mushrooms are now raised intensively in a purpose-built environment, but in this 1930s photograph, mushrooms are being picked in a meadow by the light of bicycle lamps and candles. Holes ten inches deep were dug and filled with suitable manure before the spawn was inserted. Six to ten weeks later, the mushrooms were ready, coming up virtually overnight and having to be gathered early in the morning so that they were 'morning fresh' for the shops and markets.

Some harvesting could be very cold work. These graphic photographs show something of the drudgery involved where crops still had to be pulled by hand – hands from which the feeling quickly vanished in conditions like these.

Above, in January 1956, workers on a farm near Well Hill in Kent bag up 56 lb sacks of

January King cabbages, which would have been sold to a local retailer. The January King, still available in supermarkets, was reputed to be the best of the late cabbages, large, with few outer leaves and tinged with a purple shade. On the far left: a similar scene in 1952, but this time the cabbage is a forage crop for livestock.

Maize was generally grown as green fodder or as a silage crop, which was chaffed before being packed into the silo, but here, unusually for Britain, it is the cobs that are being harvested. It is November 1948, and the workers are wearing overcoats, which appear to be veterans of wartime service.

Root crops could be stored for several months after lifting as long as they were protected from frost by layers of earth and straw in a carefully constructed clamp and the weather did not warm up, which would cause regrowth and rotting. Below: in Kent in 1954, the last of a 1,000

box clamp of long beet, representing the yield of four acres, is being packed. Above: another scene in Kent, this time in 1938, where over 100 tons of potatoes are being unclamped. Unusually, they are being graded by hand – probably because the unclamping is happening late (in May) and some of the potatoes are diseased or damaged. Normally they would have been sorted mechanically on riddles. Finally, two workers warm up with a cup of tea on a freezing December day in 1950.

Reeds

A striking example of a natural and readily available resource being harvested and put to everyday use. The large picture shows a scene at Slapton, South Devon in 1930, where the reeds provided a harvest which would eventually be despatched to all parts of the county and used chiefly to thatch the roofs of country cottages. The reeds were cut with a sharp hook or scythe, as used by the Norfolk reed cutter here, carried in large, flat-bottomed boats and finally laid out to dry in nearby fields. The harvest started in November and continued until early in April, when shoots began to appear and the marshmen left the reedbeds for fear of damaging the new crop. One man could cut 50 to 100 sheaves (or shoves as they were known in Norfolk) daily, and one sheaf would make about one square foot of new roofing.

Rural skills

Much of the charm of rural architecture was due to its distinctive local character. Craftsmen with generations of expertise developed particular styles of construction to get the best out of the materials available nearby. Thatching, for example, varied considerably from place to place depending on what materials were used. In parts of Devon, for instance, unthreshed or combed wheat straw was common, while in East Anglia thatched roofs were predominantly made of reed, which was reputed to be the best for weather tightness and longevity. Elsewhere long straw wheat, rye or oat straw, rushes or in moorland areas, heather might be used. Opposite a thatcher, working in Norfolk in 1936, is dressing a course of Norfolk reed with a tool called a leggett (a practice not applied to wheat thatching), and on the far left long straw is being drawn out for thatch in September 1939; before it can be used it has to be laid out on the ground and dampened to make it more flexible.

Below: hurdle fences being made from willow at Woodbastwick on the Norfolk Broads in August 1951. Three or four horizontal rods at a time were interwoven with upright sticks, to make an almost windproof screen for garden or farm.

In East Anglia and parts of the Home Counties, flints were used extensively in building. One aspect of the flint builder's craft is garretting – embedding flint chips in mortar joints. Where pitchers (large, natural flints) have been laid in straight level courses, the lime mortar tends to be vulnerable to frost and damp, and the flint chips act as drip points. This flint knapper, photographed in 1961 in Brandon, Suffolk, was one of only two remaining employees at a business specialising in producing gunflints. The iron hammer is used to quarter a large flint, before it is broken into smaller pieces.

The traditional rural economy embraced a rich diversity of crafts and trades which, between them, satisfied most of the material needs of the local community. During the 19th century there were many changes. The railways made new manufactured goods and cheap imports available, and many craftsmen moved away from the villages to work in newly established large workshops and factories in the market towns. But some traditional craftsmen remained, the last few surviving until about the 1940s.

Basket-making grew up in areas where there was a plentiful supply of osier or withy willow – in Somerset, East Anglia and the Kennet and Thames valleys, for example. Osiers, withies or rods were graded according to quality: green rods were cut at any time of year for the cheapest baskets, and brown rods were cut only in winter and then stored for use later. But most baskets were made from white rods or stripped willow (cut in the spring when the sap was rising) because the removal of the bark made for a better seasoned, lighter and more attractive result than could be achieved with older, unstripped, brown wood. They were used for a multitude of purposes: carrying fish or poultry, gathering and marketing fruit and vegetables, shopping, as workbaskets, as wicker crates for the transportation of bulky items, even as animal muzzles and bird cages.

The basket maker on the left in the foreground, photographed in 1948, had worked on the banks of the Severn near Apperley for forty years and is making a basket for domestic use, though his main production was of containers for fruit and coal. Basketmakers sit, as here, on the ground with their legs stretched out, and work on a lapboard. The willow must be soaked just enough to be pliable and is then woven from the base up, left to right, each new rod overlapping the previous one. The

tools used are few and simple.

Left: baskets are being made for trapping salmon and eels on the river Severn. The eel traps have a distinctive double waist, while the salmon putchers are about five feet long with an opening two feet wide tapering to a point. Above: a straw bee-skep being made by an old man photographed in the early 1930s who had learnt the craft as a boy, simply by watching an old woman in the village. It was carried on chiefly as a leisurely evening occupation, sitting in the sun outside the cottage door, after a day's work in the fields or woodlands. The wheat straw was bound tightly with split strands of hazel or willow and the last circle of the skep was finished with a wooden hoop, into which an entrance was cut for the bees. Straw bee skeps have now been replaced by more modern and scientifically designed beehives.

Woodland Crafts

By the 1940s, a few hundred independent woodland craftsmen were all that remained of what had been extensive and highly organised rural industries. Those who survived longest provided goods and services mainly for local people. So the scythe handle and rake maker had work while the hay and corn harvests remained unmechanised, and the hurdle maker faced a certain future until the demise of arable flocks and sheep folding. The Second World War gave a last, tiny boost to the craftsmen who remained, while Britain became temporarily more dependent on indigenous skills and products, but soon after the woodland industries began to die out definitively.

Bodgers, craftsmen who supplied the hand-turned components for chairs to furniture factories, were still working in the Chilterns – a traditional centre of the wood working trades – in the early 1950s. Beech was the stock material, and the usual practice was to thin out the trees in rotation every seven or eight years. On the left, a bottomer works a seat to the deep, comfortable shape of a Windsor chair, using a curved and dished adze, and, on the right, a pole lathe is being used to turn a chair leg.

Part of the fascination of the old woodland economy is that each piece of wood had its own special use, and nothing was wasted. On the right, birch twigs are being gathered for use in vinegar refining: layers of twigs were placed in the bottom of the vats to help clarify the liquid. Above, tent pegs are being made in a woodland workshop in the 1930s. Tent peg makers usually worked in pairs, because two were needed to fell the trees. The beech trunks were cut into blocks and then split using a flammer and molly (a splitting iron and mallet). The notch of the peg was then cut – the only part of the work, apart from the felling, where a saw was used – and finally the peg was shaped with a draw knife on a shavehorse, with a vice controlled by the feet. Each pile of pegs (which were stacked to dry) contained a hundred. In warm weather they were ready to use in a week, but in winter they had to remain stacked for a month. A good worker could make between 800 and 900 pegs in a day.

Laddermaking was undertaken by wheelwrights as well as by specialist hand workers in woodland workshops. Poles of larch or spruce were cut locally and, when well-seasoned, split in two, one side flat and the other rounded. Resting the poles on supports just clear of the ground, the ladder maker then bored out holes and drove oak staves into the holes, as shown here. The rungs were carefully shaped with a draw knife or spokeshave, and had to be an exact fit. The craftsman would have knocked a wooden gauge into each hole as he made it to test for size. Most ladders were fifteen to thirty feet long, and this one, made in 1948, was to be used for stack-making and thatching.

Rake makers fitted their trade to the seasonal pattern, undertaking a wide range of coppice work between times. They worked mainly with ash and hazel in small estate or private yards using hand tools and possibly a pole lathe. Here short and long (or drag) hayrakes are being made. After the poles of ash or willow have been roughly trimmed, the handles (or stails) are straightened by steam, if necessary in a setting brake. They are then fixed in a shavehorse and shaped by a draw knife, and

afterwards by a circular plane or lathe. One end of the handle is split to form the prongs. Shorter poles are used for the heads and the teeth rammed home into prepared holes. When all are in place the teeth are pointed, and the head attached to the splayed division of the handle.

Ash gate hurdles, characteristic of the midland, northern and border counties, being made in a village rather than a woodland workshop. The other type was the wattle hurdle, made of hazel, which was more common in the rest of the country.

Wheelwrights

The formidable skills of wheelwrights were in constant demand while horsepower was the principal form of transport. A well-crafted wheel, once enclosed by a metal tyre, could withstand years of jolting across fields and along rough country roads. But by the 1930s, when these photographs were taken, many fewer wheelwrights could make a living, and those who did often relied mainly on repair work. This wheelwright, however, was still making new wheels.

The hub of a wheel was almost invariably made of well-seasoned elm, the spokes of oak and the felloes, which form the outside of the

wheel, of ash or elm. Each part was precisely measured and shaped, then closely fitted to give the tightest of joints, without the use of any glue or nails.

Tyring was undertaken by specialist wheelwrights or blacksmiths. The circular iron tyre, made marginally smaller than the outer circumference of the wheel, was heated until red hot in a wood fire, then lifted by the smith with large tongs (or tyring dogs), slid over the wheel it had now expanded to fit and rapidly levered and banged into position. Copious amounts of water were poured on to prevent the wooden rim catching fire, producing billowing clouds of steam, and, as the cooling proceeded, the tyre shrank, giving off a succession of loud, cracking and clicking noises as the metal contracted, until the whole assembly was bound in a vice-like grip and reckoned roadworthy.

Village life

Until the Second World War, most villages still enjoyed the luxury of a general store. There would also – in medium-sized and large villages – have been a shoeing and general smith, whose fiery workshop was a source of great fascination to local children. Opposite, a blacksmith in Essex is forging a horseshoe on his anvil, and here a shoe is being burnt on to a horse's hoof before nailing in Lavenham, Suffolk, in 1967.

The much-vaunted tranquillity of the English countryside has now vanished from most of its villages. Above is the picturesque stone village of Wetton in North Staffordshire in the late 1920s, when it had a population of under 300. As yet, this village had been unaffected by modern developments; the road is not made up and the motor car, bringing with it trippers, tea houses, petrol pumps and roadside hoardings, has not yet arrived. Despite appearances, life was hardly idyllic. There were few amenities, and water had to be carried by hand from a spring or well. Many villages at this time were without mains water or other services until the post-war Labour government improved provision with its nationalisation programme. Even so, the more remote locations had to wait until the 1960s and 1970s for connection. On the left is the village of Bibury in Gloucestershire, which featured in many an 'olde England' postcard series. A relatively accessible place, it already had regular visitors by the mid 1930s – in 1935 it boasted two tea houses, a guest house and a hotel.

Right: a well-to-do lady still prefers horse to motorised transport in the quiet main street, Castle Coombe, Wiltshire, c.1930. Below: a picture taken in the 1930s of a flock of sheep being driven through the village after leaving Weyhill Sheep Fair, Hampshire, one of the last surviving events of this kind. In its heyday in the 18th century, Weyhill attracted well over a quarter of a million sheep for sale over the course of a week.

Rural entertainment

Country dwellers had always provided their own entertainment and continued to do so long after their city counterparts had taken to more passive recreation. Many customs and festivals could be traced back to pagan times, and behind them lay the rhythms of the seasons and the realities of the farming year. Mumming plays, which were traditionally performed at mid-winter before the spring sowing, symbolised a supplication for the regeneration of the earth and return of the sun. Guising, or the wearing of animal masks, which again originally took place in winter, recalled a belief in sympathetic magic. May Day ceremonies were intended to aid the coming of spring and linked human fertility with the increase of nature. Opposite: the newly crowned May Queen in Torrington, Devon, probably in the 1920s, before a carnival procession and dancing in the street. On the far left is a scene in Minehead, Somerset, in 1925, with the May Day hobby horse, made of painted canvas and decorated with ribbons, which was shown off while pennies were collected round the village. Probably associated with ancient fertility rites, it is also said to recall a shipwreck on May Day eve in 1722 from which the body of a cow was washed ashore. The tail was cut off, attached to the hobby, and a toll demanded from onlookers.

In the 19th century, agricultural changes, better communications and national education meant that many customs and festivals began to die out or lose much of their meaning, and efforts to preserve and revive them by middle-class Victorians met with varying degrees of success. But some still survived well into this century and remained the way in which country people marked the events of the rural calendar. Thomas Hardy remarked wryly in a novel written in 1878 that in a modern revival of a tradition the performers will appear enthusiastic, while in a genuinely surviving festival, they will seem to be carrying out their annual task out of a sense of dreary obligation.

Below: wassailing the apple trees, in Carhampton, Somerset, on Twelfth Night, 1931. Behind this superstition is the idea of driving away evil spirits which might harm the fruit. Villagers encircled the largest tree in one of the local orchards. The branches were hung with toast soaked in cider, more cider was thrown on the tree and guns were fired into the branches. An incantation was sung beginning: Old apple tree, old apple tree

We've come to wassail thee.

The Horn Dance at Abbots Bromley in Staffordshire commemorates the restoration of lost forest rights during the reign of Henry III, although the character of the dance is much older. The six leading players, acting out a hunt, carry deer skulls complete with antlers, and dance to an accordion and triangle. With them are a man dressed as Robin Hood and mounted on a hobby-horse, another representing Maid Marion, a Fool in cap and bells, and a man with crossbow and arrows. After the first dance, the deer-men proceed through the parish, visiting farmhouses and cottages, bringing good fortune to the inhabitants. Like other ritual dramas, it was enthusiastically taken up by Victorian Anglican clergy (the present costumes were designed in 1860 by the vicar's daughters to celebrate the completed restoration of the church). This photograph was taken in 1933, when the onlookers were surely locals.

The 'county set' had its own forms of entertainment. Here the Golden Retriever Club Sanction Show is being judged at Herons Buckhold, near Pangbourne, Berkshire, in June 1934. The best dog and winner of the Patiala Cup was Anningsley Fox, seen on the right of the photograph. On the right, a pheasant shoot at Bishop Burton, near York, in 1929, with working retrievers.

Hunting and shooting

Left: the first shoot of the season on an estate in North Norfolk, one year in the late 1930s. While shooting was one of the traditional pursuits of the country gentry, it was also enjoyed, when the opportunity arose, by those born and bred in villages. Below: in January 1936, local sportsmen try their hand at wildfowling on flooded moorland near Langport, Somerset.

In 1931, when the ratcatcher with his gun, ferret and dog was photographed, vermin control was still a considerable problem. Rats tended to go out into the hedgerows and fields during the summer and returned to barns and other buildings in the winter. Sometimes farmers clubbed together to hire a specialist like this one, but often a villager would be a spare-time ratcatcher and get paid by the tail. The rabbit trapper, with a good bag for a winter's day, was photographed around 1948.

An evocative sight: the South Berkshire Hunt passing a plough team while running at Ufton, Berkshire, almost certainly in the 1930s. Many villagers and farm workers would have enjoyed following the hunt on foot, or watching from strategic vantage points. But some farm workers disapproved, not least lowland shepherds, who opposed hunting on the grounds that it disturbed the sheep at lambing time. Farmers, too, might strongly dislike the horses coming over their land when it was soft, or the crops young, because of the damage done. But tenant farmers would generally not risk protesting against the activities of a hunting landlord, and independent farmers often felt compelled to tolerate it because they wanted to move in the same circles as the hunters.

Hunting remained a fashionable activity between the wars, but it suffered from the parlous economic climate and the sale of much estate land. The old county hierarchy was disappearing and many farmers could no longer afford to hunt. At the same time, the number of people who kept horses also declined as the motor car replaced the horse and carriage, and this reduced the membership of the professional classes (the doctor, solicitor and parson) as well as that of the rural tradesmen. More and more, it was the better-off, in particular those who had made their fortunes in business and industry, who took part in the hunts that survived.

Tithe protests

The 1930s saw a revival of farmers' resistance to paying tithes, a medieval system whereby one tenth of the annual produce of each parish was paid by law to the clergy. In 1836, this was reduced to a smaller rent charge, but the fact that agriculture was the only industry so taxed was bitterly resented, and, already threatened by bankruptcy, many farmers refused to pay. Thousands of court orders were issued, and attempts by auctioneers to sell farmers' goods often led to pitched battles with the authorities. When this photograph was taken at a tithe distraint sale in South Oxfordshire in June 1934, the agitation was reaching its climax. About thirty policemen, some in plain clothes, were drafted in, but the farmers' tactics changed. Instead of boycotting the sale, they bid so low that it was difficult for matters to proceed. Thirty-six Shorthorn heifers, three polled Angus cross-bred heifers and one steer were offered to meet a debt of £176. The first bid was eighteen pence for sixteen heifers.

A farmworker's home

While the countryside of sixty years ago may seem to modern eyes to have been an idyllic place to live, the accommodation provided for those who actually worked on the land was often cold, damp and comfortless, with no laid-on water or other services and usually an outside privy. Some improvements were made, but there was still a housing crisis in 1948 when this photograph was taken and presented to Parliament (along with others) as part of a campaign for better rural housing. Philip Rye and his wife and six children (all under seven) had lived in this tin shack at Crockenhill in Kent for six-and-a-half years.

Canals

It was the coming of the railways that spelt the beginning of the long decline of the canal system in Britain, and later motorised transport captured yet more of the trade that had previously been handled on the waterways. A few routes remained commercially viable until the Second World War, mainly for bulk transport of commodities such as coal. Horse dung from the towns was traditionally transported back to the country by canal, but this came to an end once horse power was no longer important in the towns and artificial fertilisers had been developed. By the end of the war, many previously busy canals had become pleasant backwaters, rich in wild flowers and wildlife. Some had fallen into disuse altogether, and through want of puddling (maintaining the clay bottom) and proper upkeep had lost their water. But both of these photographs, containing working barges, were taken in the 1950s.

On the left is the Wey, a semi-canalised navigation between Guildford and Weybridge which gave access to the London Docks via the Thames. On the Wey, horses continued to provide the means of haulage until 1960. Most Wey barges, with a capacity of 80 tons, required two Shire horses each, working in tandem. An important feature, which can be seen here, was the large wooden rudder and tiller. The towing post is at the fore end, as is the anchor, used for mooring in the tideway. The man in charge of the horses has moved to the wrong side of the team to give the photographer a better view. The trace chain on the second horse would usually have been prevented from causing chafing by the use of painted wooden bobbins threaded on to the chain; in this case sacking has been used to the same end.

On this page is a stretch of the northern section of the Oxford canal, photographed in 1953, when the Docks and Inland Waterways Executive had recommended that this canal be kept in commercial use. Others were transferred to local authorities for pleasure boating and other recreational purposes.

Gypsies

Some gypsies wandered the length of Britain, while others kept to a particular locality. It was not unusual for some gypsies to 'go indoors' during the winter months and to spend the summer travelling: fruit, potato or pea picking, plying some roadside craft, selling door to door, or visiting one of the numerous fairs or other meetings of travelling folk. This family from Wiltshire lived in a village over the winter and camped out on the downs for the summer, carrying on the traditional trade of peg-making, though by the time this picture was taken in 1958, few housewives wanted old-fashioned hand-made wooden clothes pegs; other traditional skills, such as basket-making, also became redundant and, as the availability of seasonal piecework on farms declined, scrap-metal dealing became the great residual occupation.

A traditional horsedrawn bow-top van and a woman typically dressed in a tight-waisted, full skirt, blouse and silk scarf fastened by a brooch. Her braided hair has been made stiff and shiny with soapy water or with mutton fat or butter. The dog, a lurcher, is also characteristic. Below: gypsies on the move in January 1934, packing up their possessions on the Romany settlement, which had been at Hurtwood Hill, near Guildford, Surrey, for nearly a century. Over 300 are leaving their benders (huts made of bent willow branches covered with sacks) to begin new lives in three-roomed, corrugated iron, bungalows in Walton-on-Thames. A culture based on gypsy pride and the horse was in decline as the old occupations withered. The new were based on the debris of the industrial age, and encampments became strewn with junk. Concern about rural living standards and children's education led to an increasing campaign in the 1930s to sanitise and settle the lives of travelling folk.

Sheep and shepherds

Traditionally, there were three broad categories of sheep farming. In upland areas, mainly in the north, Wales and Scotland, sheep were bred and grazed where the land made cultivation awkward or impossible – a practice which continues today. In the south, too, there were grassland flocks kept on land suitable only for pasture or on land laid down to grass for a few years. But on light arable land, especially in the east and the south, so-called arable sheep were moved from field to field during at least part of the winter, feeding on specially grown crops of turnips or swede and kale grown in alternate strips. By the spring, the ground had been enriched with fine quality manure and was ready to produce a good yield of corn. This was the classical English way of improving light land. In the summer, the sheep would be grazed on grassland such as the South Downs or on clover or vetches quickly grown between main crops. But this beautifully integrated and balanced system of husbandry was not to survive. The cost of growing labour-intensive crops of roots for sheep to feed on in winter became prohibitive, and the old arable breeds such as Hampshire Downs began to disappear.

By the late 1930s, most flocks raised in southern England were grassland sheep cross-bred to mature early and give fat lambs. Opposite: in-lamb Dorset Down ewes are being brought down from their grazing to the shelter of the lambing pens on the lower ground.

Right: Jimmy Dunford, one of the last shepherds in charge of an arable flock, standing guard over his snow-bound sheep on Salisbury Plain in a blizzard in December 1937. Below: a North Country shepherd gives his flock of Herdwicks a few wisps of hay. This seems small nourishment, but hill sheep are hardy creatures and well adapted to the severe climate of the districts in which they are found. The value of a native flock, which generally knows the boundaries of its often extensive grazing area as precisely as the shepherd, is such that an incoming farmer would pay well above what he would give in the open market for similar sheep.

With Downs sheep under arable conditions, as here, the usual lambing time was February. An elaborate lambing pen would be built, from hurdles windproofed with straw, and with more straw nearby for litter. The shepherd would move into the hut he would live in during the lambing season (made of wood or corrugated iron and containing a coal stove, a bunk and often a medecine chest) and bring all his tackle, including troughs and hay-racks, in good time for lambing to begin.

Shepherds often believed in their own remedies for ailments and disease in sheep. But

the best men, like Ted Jackson, shown above in 1951, were reputed to have a wonderful way with animals and reckoned to save more lambs by patience, warmth and whisky than by any other means. Ted disapproved of destroying animals if there was any chance of treating them and was also opposed to what he held to be unnatural methods of farming, such as artificial fertilisers, which he was sure undermined animals' health. On the right, a shepherd holds twin lambs not by the legs, as some did, risking damage, but safely against his body.

Sheep washing before clipping. It was disputable whether washing sheep was worth the effort. Clean wool fetched a higher price, but without the dirt the fleece weighed less. By the late 1940s, the practice was becoming less common; sheep grazed on grass rarely got as dirty as arable sheep. Opposite are pedigree Hampshire Downs being washed in the Kennet, near Ramsbury in Wiltshire, and the picture on the left shows a less orthodox way of dunking sheep, by pushing them into the river Ure by the bridge at West Tanfield near Ripon in Yorkshire. Both pictures date from the 1930s. At the Cenarth Fells, in Carmarthenshire, in 1960, a fisherman with a coracle helps with the process.

Sheep must be shorn at the time they tend naturally to shed their fleeces. This is called the rise in the wool, and it occurs earlier in the south of the country (May or early June) than in the north. Shortly after shearing (and again in the autumn) the lambs and ewes are dipped to rid them of parasites.

Opposite, a flock is being tackled by a team of shearers at Howgill near Sedbergh in the West Riding in July 1946. A skilled man with hand shears can shear four sheep an hour, at

Even as recently as the 1950s, it was not unusual in some parts of the country for livestock to be driven through the streets of a market town if that was the most direct route for them. This upland flock, shown in Kendal, belongs to farmers in Upper Wensleydale, whose habit it had long been to send their Swaledales down to overwinter in the more sheltered pastures around Windermere. Some 500 to 600 sheep, here on the final lap of their journey, have covered forty miles in a couple of days.

most forty a day, whereas a man with electric shears can cope with about three to four times as many.

On the right is a Westmorland shearing scene in the 1950s. Hand shears are still being used on a flock of Rough Fells. This skill persisted among hill farmers, who liked to leave a good deal of wool on the sheep as protection against rough weather. It also survived among shearing gangs who went from farm to farm in some districts.

Harvest-time

Of all the farming activities in the year, harvest provided perhaps the hardest yet most satisfying work. Now the farmer quite literally reaped the rewards of his labours. Traditional methods were slow by comparison with the speed of modern combines, and it was easy to fall victim to the vagaries of the weather.

Here a labourer is opening up a field of wheat with a scythe and cradle or 'bender' near Shoreham in Kent during the 1947 harvest. This allows a binder to get round the field so that it can start cutting without going through the standing corn. Another worker alongside the scythesman will tie the corn gathered and swept to one side by the cradle. This, or awkward corners of corn that had

been beaten down or laid by bad weather, were by now the only jobs for a scythesman. Once modern combine harvesters with cutters at the front of the machine had come in, from about 1950, the need for the task was eliminated completely.

On the left, a fine crop of seed clover is being harvested, raked into rows and pitched into the cart, which will take it to be threshed in a clover huller. Clover, often mixed with grasses, was grown in rotation with other arable crops in a system which enhanced the fertility of the land as well as providing rich fodder. Above: cutting a field of oats by binder with three strapping teams of Clydesdales at Arrat Farm, near Brechin, Angus, in August 1960, when there were still some 70,000 binders working. The binder, which cut, gathered and tied corn into sheaves, had replaced the earlier reaper as the chief means of harvesting corn by about the time of the Great War. By the mid 1960s it had itself been almost entirely superseded by the combine harvester which cut, gathered and threshed the corn in one operation.

In August 1949 the country was still short of food following the war, and extra workers were needed to bring in the considerable harvest that had resulted from the wartime plough-up campaign. Many townspeople at this time chose to combine their holidays with harvest work in the cornfields. In the background is the campsite of these Londoners enjoying the open air in Somerset. Farmers had mixed feelings about the employment of holidaymakers, especially if they had to pay them the agricultural rate, as instructed by the government, but often they had no other source of help. The inexperience of this group shows in their bared arms, which will quickly become scratched and sore.

In the photograph opposite is a crop of oats on a farm near Canterbury in 1954, when much of England suffered bad weather that lasted the whole summer – probably the reason why the stooks look a bit flattened. The whole field will need to be restooked; otherwise there is a risk that the ears will touch the ground, allowing the corn to sprout, making it virtually useless. An everyday landscape when the picture was taken, this rich-looking vista of stooked corn and hedgerows surrounding oasthouses nestling in the valley is truly a sight of the past.

Harvesting flax: not the favourite task of farm-workers as the coarse stems had to be pulled out by their roots if the crop was to be used for its fibre (ultimately to be made into linen thread), as here. As well as being tedious and back-breaking, the job was very hard on the hands. Here the crop is being stood up in small, loose sheaves, the roots end well spread out so that air can circulate freely and prevent any heating or fermentation which could damage the fibres. Flax was also grown for its seed (linseed) which was fed to cattle in winter.

A picturesque scene just after eight o'clock in the evening near Windermere in the Lake District in July 1940: the day's work is almost over. After the coils or cocks of hay have been left to dry or 'make' for a few days, they are loaded on a cart. One man is raking down the load after it has been roped and before it goes on the road.

The best hay, which should be a greenish colour, is made under a bright but not too hot sun, without too much handling. In Scotland and the north of England, it was common to put the mown grass in large heaps, which protected it to some extent from rain; then it was collected once it had had a chance to dry out or 'sweat'. But more settled weather conditions in the south made hay-making easier, and it was gathered straight from the field to the rick.

Haylofts were occasionally a source of great delight to children who, when the farmer wasn't looking, would do death-defying leaps from the rafters on to the huge cushion of hay below. In the photograph on the far left, hay is being pitched into the top of a hayloft or tallet above a stable, probably to feed horses below.

Below: building a rick in 1939 at Purley, near Reading. The hay wagon has just arrived and the horse waits patiently while hay is unloaded on to the elevator, which is almost certainly being powered by a small oil engine. Scenes like this have now disappeared from the farmed landscape, as nearly all hay is now packed in large circular bales, which are lifted by a tractor with a front-loading attachment and placed on a specially designed trailer to be transported back to the farm buildings.

Here, harvesters are setting up stooks on a ten-acre field on the banks of the river Dee in August 1965. First a couple of sheaves – one in each hand – were taken by the head. Next the butts were dropped on to the ground so that the two rested against each other. Then more were added, commonly six to eight, sometimes as many as ten or twelve, but always an even number as an odd sheaf placed at one end would prevent the free circulation of air, and then there would be a risk of rotting. Once the binder was replaced by the combine, which cut and threshed the grain in a single action, the stooking of corn was no longer necessary.

Opposite: break time for no fewer than fifteen harvesters in a wheat field in the Thames Valley. The horses are all wearing shaft harness, which means that carting has started. The boys' task will be to lead the horses between the stooks as they are gathered up. The young man with the gun, probably the farmer's son, will shoot at rabbits escaping from the stooks. Hobnail boots are still being worn, making this almost certainly a pre-war photograph.

Half-wet, half-dry: stooked and stacked oats on a farm at Pitlochry in Perthshire, after a wet harvest in 1964. Stacking oats or hay on tripods made from pieces of wood lashed together was common in the north of England and Scotland. The idea was to protect the stack from the effects of rain by allowing as much sun and wind as possible to get at it.

A quintessential scene of high summer: carting on an estate in the Thames Valley in the 1930s. Two men are pitching wheat sheaves on to the harvest wagon, and a third is loading. Fitting ladders to both ends of the wagon has increased its capacity to between 100 and 120 sheaves. You can just see the boy in charge of the horse standing by its forelegs, and the coiled rope for securing the load at the rear of the wagon. In the background another lost feature of the landscape: a line of fine elms. Left: a waterlogged harvest in late August 1944.

Thatching a wheat stack in Gloucestershire in 1947. Most medium to large farms had a worker who was able to turn his hand to this job. Oblong stacks were more common in the south of England and round stacks in the north. The tractor is a Fordson Major with spade lugs, rather than rubber tyres, which were still difficult to get, even after the war, and a trailer containing fuel and spares. Below is a group of impeccably neat, hip-ended ricks (oblong with rounded ends) on an estate farm at Englefield in Berkshire, standing on iron staddles to keep vermin out.

Hop Harvest

The great tradition of Londoners going down to Kent to help with the hop harvest goes back at least to the mid 19th century. In London's East End, going hopping was a way of getting out into the country for people who would otherwise probably not have thought of having a holiday. Above is Mrs Hall of Stepney, who had been a hop picker for forty years when this picture was taken in 1956. Picking started early in September and lasted about three weeks. Most of the pickers were women or children, but sometimes whole families were employed. On the left, pickers are stripping the hops from the bines and putting them into bins, wooden frameworks covered by sacking. The measurer will scoop the hops into the bushel basket; each bushel will be noted in a ledger by the booker and then emptied into a loosely packed poke or green bag (containing 10-12 bushels) for transport to the kiln.

In the other great area for hops, Herefordshire and Worcestershire, where this photograph was taken just before the war, oast houses were known as hop kilns.

In Kent again, slum kids from the East End play in one of the alleys next to the hops, which are on wirework, the usual system of supporting hop plants by this time. The earlier method involved stringing hops on individual poles.

Inside a Worcestershire hop kiln in 1934. The hop dryer was the most important person involved in the harvest, for it was he who ensured that the hops dried evenly, that the fires were at the right temperature and that the hops were cured to the right texture. He used a blunt-tined fork to avoid damaging them. After drying, the hops, which are very fragile at this stage, are laid out on the floor of the cooling loft to equalise their moisture content until they become tougher and more suitable for pressing. They are then rammed tightly into large pockets with a hop press, and are ready to be despatched.

The first hop-picking machine was introduced in 1934, but few farmers used machines to begin with because mechanically picked hops were more difficult to dry. Nowadays the bines are still cut down manually, but from a tractor-drawn trailer, and they are then taken to a picking plant where machines can strip 1000 bines per hour.

Hops require a constant flow of heated air to dry properly, and from the 18th century oasthouses were adapted to incorporate the now familiar cone or pyramidal roof, about fifteen or twenty feet high, ending in a circular opening and often topped by a wooden cowl, which was pivoted away from the wind. In the days before oasthouses were fitted with fans, the cone acted as a giant flue producing a natural draught. Here a wagon arrives at a hopyard near Ledbury in Herefordshire and unloads pokes for drying.

Threshing

Threshing oats in a Kentish field in August 1933, with the uncut cereal visible behind the water cart. After the harvest had been cut, using a binder, the grain still had to be separated from the straw and loaded into sacks. Usually corn was threshed from the stack in the autumn and winter months when grain prices were relatively good. In the depths of the depression, the farmer must have been really hard up to thresh straight from the harvest in the summer,

when the market was glutted and his grain was likely to fetch only about half the price it would have earned later in the year. The thresher here is driven by a Marshall engine. There is no elevator and it is likely that the man leaning on the fork is waiting for another wagonload of oats to arrive which he will then pitch up to the men on top of the thresher. The windshield protects them from the breeze. The straw is being tied and then tossed into the wagon, before being taken back to the farm.

Threshing barley at Upton in Berkshire in the early 1930s. Two men, the un-rickers, are standing on the corn rick, immediately behind the horse, and are pitching on to the thresher. The job is nearly finished and the foreman has come on to the rick to help with the last sheaves. There are two further men on the thresher, one of whom is cutting the bands on the sheaves, while the other feeds the barley into the threshing drum. At the back end of the machine, on the left of the photograph, the threshed corn is being bagged in two cwt sacks and loaded on the wagon, which is drawn by a nice team of matched horses, suggesting that this is an estate farm. An elevator carries the straw from the drum to the straw stack, where two more men are building it. An International Harvester 10/20 provides the power to drive the thresher and the bonnet has been left open in a hopeful attempt to keep the engine cool. The elevator is powered by the thresher. Note the once common elms in the background, which will almost certainly have perished from Dutch Elm Disease in the epidemic of the 1960s and 1970s.

On a farm near Bognor Regis, Sussex, in late March 1947, where threshing has been delayed because of appalling weather. Two Land Girls in this threshing gang are cleaning chaff and fragments of straw away from the thresher – a particularly dirty and unpopular job. In the mid foreground is the man bagging off the grain with a sack trolley beside him. The roll of wire netting was supposed to be around the stack to keep rats away. Right: children with gas masks over their shoulders watching threshing in progress at Westerham in Kent in September 1939, the first month of the Second World War. The traction engine shown here was made by the local firm of Aveling and Porter of Rochester.